The
GayBCs

**For Braylor,
and for every kid who wonders**

Library of Congress Cataloging in Publication Number: 2019936799

ISBN: 978-1-68369-162-4

Printed in China
Typeset in Gilroy and Century Schoolbook
Designed by Aurora Parlagreco
Production management by John J. McGurk

Quirk Books
215 Church Street
Philadelphia, PA 19106
quirkbooks.com

10 9 8 7 6 5 4 3 2 1

The GayBCs

Words and Pictures by

M. L. Webb

QUIRK BOOKS
PHILADELPHIA

is for **ALLY.**
A friend who is there
to stand up for you
with strength, love, and care.

is for **BI.**
You can shout it out loud:
"I like boys *and* girls,
and that makes me proud!"

is for **COMING OUT.**
You're ready to share
what you feel deep inside;
it's okay to be scared.

is for **DRAG.**
You can strut and dance
in clothes that you love:
dresses, heels, or pants!

is for **EQUALITY.**
We're on the same team!
We all have the right
to love, hope, and dream.

is for **FAMILY.**
Related or found,
they'll stick by your side
through your ups and downs.

is for **GAY.**
It's a word that implies
you're a girl who likes girls
or a guy who likes guys.

is for **HOPE.**
Dream up a life you'll love.
The sky is the limit;
shoot for the stars above!

is for **INTERSEX.**
Some are born with the parts
of both a boy and a girl;
bodies are works of art!

is for **JOY.**
You can sing, dance, and play.
Find moments of sunshine
in each and every day.

is for **KIKI.**
When friends come together
to catch up on news,
gossip, and weather.

is for **LESBIAN.**
It's love and affection
between two special girls
who share a connection.

is for **MOUNTAIN.**
The peaks that you'll move
with courage and strength
found deep inside you.

is for **NON-BINARY.**
You don't identify
as just being a girl
or just being a guy.

is for **ORIENTATION.**
It's a balance between
who you are, who you love,
and how you want to be seen.

is for **PAN.**
You connect with a vibe.
No matter the gender,
it's about what's inside.

is for **QUEER.**
An inclusive term.
It's used to show pride,
unite, and affirm!

is for **RESPECT.**
It's the right decision
to treat everyone fairly;
make it your mission.

is for **SASHAY.**
A confident, fierce stride
to show yourself off
with attitude and pride.

is for **TRANS.**
It's a brave step to take
to live as the gender
you know is innate.

is for **UNIQUE.**
There's no one like you.
Embrace who you are,
and love what you do!

is for **VOGUE.**
Time to strike a pose;
dance to the music,
and put on a show!

is for **WONDER.**
With so much to know,
always ask questions
to think, learn, and grow.

is for **X.**
You can write it down
when you don't prefer
"M" or "F" as your noun.

is for **YOU.**
Brave, creative, and strong.
You are special and loved,
and you'll always belong.

is for **ZEST.**
Be bold and live free.
Magic awaits you,
whoever you'll be!

GLOSSARY

ALLY

A person or group of people who support and stand up for another person or group.

ASEXUAL

A spectrum of identities that explores attraction or lack thereof.

BISEXUAL

Those who love and are attracted to people of two genders.

COMING OUT

When someone realizes who they are attracted to or how they identify, and they want to share that with others.

DRAG

The act of dressing up as a way to perform gender.

EQUALITY

The idea that everyone deserves to be treated the same, regardless of differences.

FAMILY

A group of people who love and care about one another, whether they are relatives or friends.

GAY

Those who love or are attracted to people of the same gender as their own.

HOPE

To want something to happen and believe that it's possible.

INTERSEX

When someone is born with some body parts that boys are expected to have, and some body parts that girls are expected to have, or sometimes neither.

JOY

A feeling of great happiness.

KIKI

A party for friends to relax and enjoy one another's company.

LESBIAN

A woman who loves and is attracted to other women.

MOUNTAIN

A large structure—physical or metaphorical—that one can climb.

NON-BINARY

A person who does not feel that the words "girl" or "boy" fit with how they describe themselves. They may feel like both a boy and a girl, or they may feel like neither a boy or a girl. Non-binary people may use pronouns such as "they," "them," or "ze" and "hir," rather than he/him or she/her.

ORIENTATION

Who a person loves or is attracted to.

PAN

The ability to fall in love or be attracted to someone regardless of their gender.

QUEER
A word used to identify with and celebrate people of all gender identities, as well as all the ways people love each other.

RESPECT
To treat someone with kindness and show you care about them.

SASHAY
To walk in a slow, confident way that makes people take notice.

TRANS
A person whose sense of personal and gender identity does not match the sex they were assigned at birth.

UNIQUE
Someone or something that is special and unlike anything else.

VOGUE
A dance style that imitates the poses that are struck by a model on a runway.

WONDER
To be curious or want to know about something.

X
A letter that can be used when someone does not identify as male (M) or female (F).

YOU
A sense of self. You can learn more about who you are over time!

ZEST
A feeling of enthusiasm and excitement.

ACKNOWLEDGMENTS

This book would not have been possible without the love and support of my wonderful partner Stephan, who always made sure that I had all the time, space, and take-out needed to work. Thank you for the constant advice and allowing me to cover our walls in sketches and illustrations over and over again. I couldn't have done this without you.

Thank you to my dear friends and family, especially my brother Josh and nephew Braylor. Without you two, I would never have thought to make such a book!

Thank you to Elana Roth Parker, my amazing agent, who took a chance on me, my art, and my story. Thanks for keeping it real.

And lastly, thanks to the powerhouse team at Quirk Books, whom I was thrilled to get to work with. Special thanks to Alex Arnold and Nicole De Jackmo for knowing just what to do with a little LGBTQ+ picture book!